white paint
flying

white paint flying

joan cofrancesco

authorHOUSE®

AuthorHouse™
1663 Liberty Drive
Bloomington, IN 47403
www.authorhouse.com
Phone: 1 (800) 839-8640

Published by AuthorHouse 02/03/2016

ISBN: 978-1-5049-7799-9 (sc)
ISBN: 978-1-5049-7800-2 (e)

"There is no beauty without some strangeness."

—edgar allen poe

remnant of red wine
one last trisket

snow in syracuse
what else is new

sunrise
on the bird feeder

moon on
cats head
as she drinks
water from
the dripping
faucet

"to get
to brooklyn
from manhattan
we have
to go under
the east
river" she said
"do you mind?"

first
i ate a brownie
then i
cut up
some poems

he said
"my kid
was playing
on the internet
the next day
i got a
bill
for $55.00
for
zombie
brains"

muse
guardian
angel
and holy spirit
all fighting
for my sleepy cat's
attention

i watch
a cat
watching
a muskrat
while the
erie canal
watches us all

love both
inspires and distracts—
i keep you
at a distance
while i hold you
in my arms

at the casino

watching
flashing colored
lights
in the night
of the living dead

riding the D
to the
brooklyn museum
to see
basquait
who used to
graffiti
these trains

used bookstore in brooklyn

a black cat
dreaming
beside a first edition
of
apollinaire

listening to beethoven
piano sonata #31
when he
suddenly
jumps to jazz

the night the lady bowlers came
to dominic's

they entered
like they owned the place
shirts embroidered
with the names of teams
one of the big ones
comes up to me at the bar
and asks "hey baby
where can a woman
get some action in this town?"

horndog

20
always horny
& creative
& growing into
my genius

among intestines
spleens bones
& formaldehyde stink
i can still
daydream

i wish i could quit
writing poetry
but then
the wind comes
and blows ripples
across the water

mangia you say

you gently
pull that
spaghetti between
your thick lips
& make me
want to come

in florence
i thought
the uffi would grab me
but it was that
spotted dalmation
sitting in the doorway
of a store
trying to paw
a fly

i could be this
cat sleeping on
a couch
in a bookstore
in new paltz
on a rainy
afternoon

i sit quietly
watching my candle
waxing poetic

my book of poems
arrived 2 days ago
the sea is calm

ulysses grabs me
by different passages
each time through

you are my
medieval village
in italy

sunday morning
your naked thigh
religion

after shoveling
i come in
my body warms
to vivaldi

even the clouds
sing
to chagall

she'd rather play
monopoly
than draw

fountain pen
haiku
about you
naked
next to me—
doodles

a simple life
with books
cats
a small garden

i wait
for bukowski's
next book
even though
he's dead

your love grows
less and less
like the rivers
in a chinese painting

beside you
i cuddle
in a thunderstorm

she gets into her baby blue
datson 280Z
muscular thighs
long brown hair
not even a wave
to the balcony

you are
a dekooning woman
all teeth
no soul

i handel
i haiku
i occult assemblages
of girls faces
tram tickets
cards
newspaper clips
i black cats
and woodstoves

wcw
doctor
poet
dancing naked
in his house

why was
her red mg
always
in the garage

hot rum
snow
falling slowly
outside henrietta
hudson's windows
on the sidewalks
of ny

naked
pouring outside
listening to mahler

tics
as the psychic
turns over
death

syracuse snowstorm
how far
the dog star sirius
is from earth

watching the dance
of the dead
as i drink
my manhattan
cremation next

the grey wolf
sleeps under my bed
my hand
slides down
and feels his
fur

rainbow
embroidered
on your faded
jean jacket
is so
60's silly
sexy

december moon
pulling the train
through green norwegian firs
glistening with snow
to nyc

urinals
and soupcans
right next to
renoir

hot bath
saturday night
black cat
staring at me
wacking an occasional
lavender bubble

in my
glass slippers
missing my wicked
stepsisters

enlightenment

i tried to be
like li po
i shaved my head
gave up all my
possessions
wore a robe and sandals
sat on a cushion
on top of a mountaintop
and meditated
but i got lonely
missed people and my cat and
syracuse university
basketball

he had one leg
and hated poetry
that's how i knew
the ghost of rimbaud
was wandering around
my apartment

my cell phone
is lost somewhere
in my bed and
my cat is purring
i think of you

"but i couldn't stand
the smell of paint"
said the poet

i think andy was lonely
with his factory
full of people

a real bat
swoops into the audience
at the theater
during *dracula*

we came together
to abbey road

a good poem
smells of lavender
and dirt
and sex
and especially
elsewhere

9 stray cats
each with 9 lives
lay around me
on the bed
as i listen
to howlin wolf

i want to be driven
van gogh in arles
picasso in paris
haring when he knew
his time was short
i want to live

i wake up
drink coffee
eat o'hara's
lunch poems again

a monkess
from tibet
i lite votive
candles

as i rake leaves
my orange cat watches
from the window

with the artwork
of keith haring
and the poetry
of prevert
i make
my own calendar

amongst your poetry
art books
duke ellington
silk persian scarfs
let's have sake
and love our shadows

alone on christmas
eating a
peanut butter &
jelly sandwich
drinking a beer
feeling like
an ancient dynasty poem

one night with you
instead i spent
eternity wondering
what
it would have been
like

bukowski
and his cat
shitting
fucking
drinking
geniuses

watching the bills
lose again
smoky bar
sunday afternoon
a certain magic
in my wine

i write in my journal
by the fireplace
my cat's muddy paw
signs my poem

you were walking
your jack russell
across wescott street
i should have known then
it wouldn't work

poetry rejection
letter
becomes
origami
cat

reading lowell's *notebooks*
wine
fire
cat on my lap

i search for you
like cats seek shade
from the hot noon sun

sometimes
my life feels
like a dream
sequence
in a david lynch flick
and other times
i feel like i'm out of my mind

deer on 81
disappearing into the woods—
how sensible!

i have fewer possessions
since i started drinking
expensive wine

i read rilke
drink absinthe
in paris

you live in santa fe
with your cat
and your music
wearing those nine-dollar
red converse sneakers

listening to lucy
in the sky
black light
pot
frankincense
our tongues
entwined

happiness

janis
in her psychedelic porsche
drinking
southern comfort
speeding
through the streets
of l.a.

my nine black cats
watch me bathing
in dead sea salts
i am all the colors
of my stained glass window

licking
your lipstick
off my wine glass

used bookstore
we cat fight over
a first edition
of baudelaire

in my open mustang
vivaldi
moonrise over
pegasus gas sign

ray johnson
dada of bunnies
pop of mail art

at the dinosaur barbeque
a biker named jesus
drinking wine

i lite
sabbath candles
so then when you come
you will glow

champagne
candles
rose petals
hearts

this beats
all the other holidays
hands down

rainy afternoon
missing cat poster
on a telephone pole
looks like lorca
the cat i just took in
but i ain't tellin'

reading *war and peace*
everyone is asleep

my poem
just got accepted
in the harvard
gay and lesbian review
let's fuck

4th of july
me in
water's edge
strauss
fireworks

as a bookmark
for my *collected*
haikus of yosa buson
i use a
massive red
maple leaf

my lover said
it's basic logic
i love u hence
i want to fuck u
up the ass

Printed in the United States
By Bookmasters